DIVINE

Divine

Poems, Meditations, and Prayers

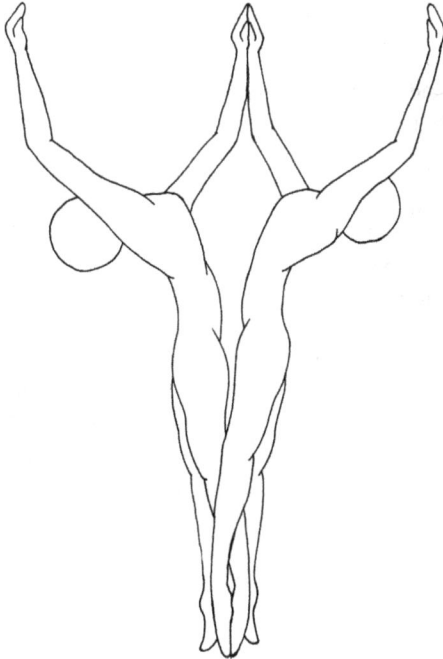

A. Guillemot

FOREWORD BY

John Moffatt

ILLUSTRATIONS BY

A. Kingfisher

RESOURCE *Publications* · Eugene, Oregon

DIVINE
Poems, Meditations, and Prayers

Resource Publications
An Imprint of Wipf and Stock Publishers
199 W. 8th Ave., Suite 3
Eugene, OR 97401

www.wipfandstock.com

PAPERBACK ISBN: 978-1-7252-8139-4
HARDCOVER ISBN: 978-1-7252-8138-7
EBOOK ISBN: 978-1-7252-8140-0

11/04/20

For Ama. For Iris. For Danaë.

A.M.D.G.

Truth is in the ashes where life burns brightly.

CONTENTS

Free Spirit: A Book of Poems

Pilgrimage: A Book of Meditations

Prayers

Foreword

On 'Divine'

IF THERE IS ANY reality to the divine, it is not to be found in books and formulae and the repetition of antique practices, though these can be both a record of past discoveries and signposts towards new ones. It is to be found in the utterly honest engagement with self and world and in a recovery of that primal longing for truth and love and transcendence which is older than any of the religions of the world. It is there that the light of revelation and the darkness of infinite silence are to be found in ways that transform us, reshape our selves, draw us closer to becoming truly human before the truly divine.

It has been my privilege to accompany A.Guillemot at one or two staging posts on the journey that shapes the writings of this book. We find in them his deeply authentic testament to the realities such a journey entails: the abandonment of old selves and familiar ways of thinking, the confrontation with darkness and chaos, the overwhelming and redeeming power of light, the pain and joy of new beginnings, and the powerful call to love and compassion in our engagement with the world and its people.

The meditations of the second part are set against the backdrop of a pilgrimage through the mountains of Norway. The raw beauty of creation is a medium for encounter with the divine, but so too is the intimacy of human love and the wonder of a new child, with which the poems are laced. Running throughout the whole is the intimation of a joyful apocalypse shot through with the hope of immortality, in which the old will pass away and a new way of being before God and with one another will set us free.

John Moffatt SJ

Preface

This is a book of religious writing for people of all faiths, and of none. It describes, first in poetry, then in prose, the relationship between ourselves as human beings and all that which is greater than ourselves, by which we are contained; here called God.

The God of this book does not judge or govern, nor bring salvation, nor stand by, idle. The God of this book is the one we meet in those moments where the true dimensions of our lives are revealed to us; those moments of honesty and vision where we become conscious of who we are. This book attempts to capture in words my own encounters with God, and the revelations that have brought me from a position of atheistic scepticism to a state of faith, over the course of ten years.

The book is divided into three sections. *Free Spirit* is a collection of poems which describe my own religious experiences. The verse forms are simple, and the language is straightforward; I hope that those who do not often read works of poetry will find them accessible. *Pilgrimage* is a collection of prose texts inspired by a journey on foot over the Norwegian mountains. The final section is comprised of short prayers.

In publishing this book, I hope to offer an intelligent, sensitive challenge to our notions of religious belief and unbelief, and to inspire others to reflect on their own spiritual practice.

A.Guillemot

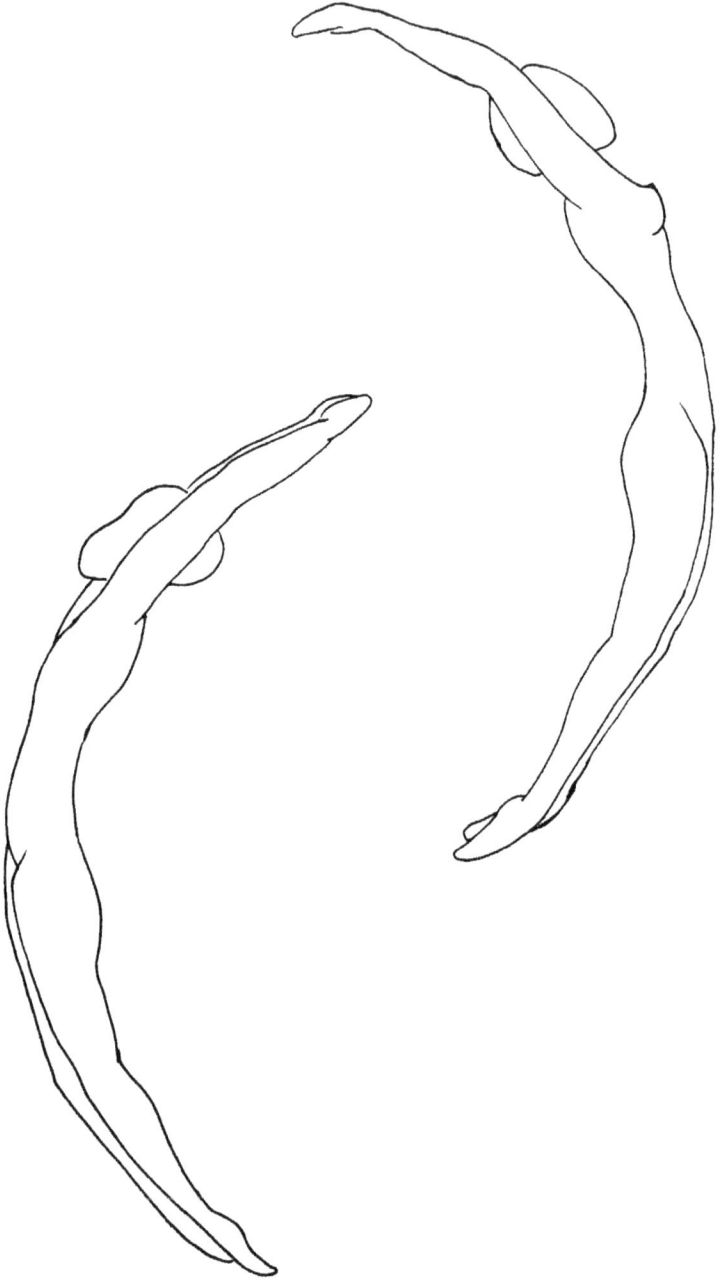

FREE SPIRIT

A Book of Poems

You Came

You came, and I awoke from dreamless sleep;
You parted my skin and breathed new life in me.
I trembled as a prayer beyond words
Scorched my tongue; raging powers
Burned in my chest. You tore from me
All that I clung on to and made me pure:
Reduced me to the elements from which I was made.
Your embrace lasted a second, lasted an hour;
And when you left me, I found I could love again.

New Life

New life stirs.
A spirit stirs
In that tired chest.
Light spills
From that heavy gaze.
Gently as a lotus,
The fist unfurls;
The creases of its palm
A crumpled map of longing.

Our fingers weave together;
Two cold heartbeats quicken.
Love flares up, makes us human.
Our new life stirs.

Resurrection

Resurrection of hope
Kicks and stirrings in the womb
The spirit seeps back into the flesh
Like firelight through the eyes and skin.

An easter resurrection:
A dying faith rekindled
To rise over a forest
Of crosses carved from memory.

On that sunlight's broad horizon,
A dream of new life shimmers.
We stand together, filled with wonder.

Love's gaze rests on us, all-knowing,
As you turn to me, and whisper:

"Listen."

"God is still alive."

Still

Still: the storm-lashed coast.
The waves breathe, wordless,
All truths spoken; flung high
Into the thin air, for wind
To lift on her palms and scatter.

Still: the two who stand.
Thoughts trace the flight of birds
Circling silently.
Arms held wide, they pray;
Lifting their horizons,
Wings spread over mountains.

Still: the evening haze,
The cathedral sky.
All prayers said, the ocean breathes
Into the silence of faithful hearts,
As they stand
Listening for an answer.

Rivers in the Dark

Like rivers in the dark, our lives
Are filled with wordless song:

Water made of names
Flows freely through our lives.

Listen in the endless song;
Stand on the banks, to hear:

Hear the night alive
With names and wordless song.

Music fills the perfect silence.
The night's alive. The night's alive.

By My Side

A dream cradles you softly – sleep by my side.
On your cheek rests the night's fallen feather.
Your lips, a crescent of sorrowful pride,
You breathe sweet as warm wind through the heather.

Is yours a beautiful dream from which you'll sigh to wake?
Tomorrow's ache in your chest? Your deepest wish blessed
By a merciful god? A snowflake
Drifting through cloudless skies as you rest?

A dream cradles you softly – sleep by my side.
You walk like a ghost through the meadows:
Where the day's rolled back its sunlit tide,
Your spirit wanders, wrapped in silken shadows.

A merciful god is here with me tonight.
You shine in his gaze; an aura of peace
Flows from your body like firelight,
As you go free through a world of dreamed release.

Your dreams rise on the night's tide.
Sleep by my side.

Dream

Dreamt of rolling grassland, boundless sky,
And leaves that danced on singing wind.
Travelled over trackless ground,
By sun and moon, through night and day.

As I walked, I spoke with God:
Told my secrets, shared my fears.
My heart grew light and shed its tears;
And then, as I fell still, God said . . .

Woke in fever; dazed, heart pounding;
Helpless, watched the visions fade.
But then, head bowed, I knelt and prayed –
And in my heart I heard God's words resounding.

Paradise

When I was a boy, I had an idea
Of a land where the water was pure and clear;
Of a land where the trees reach up, tall and proud,
Towards a gold sun wrapped in a white silk cloud.

I'd close my eyes and that sun would rise,
And I'd stand there, alone, in paradise
As the birds of the morning burst into song;
And I'd say in my heart: this is where you belong.

When I told my mother about that strange land,
She knelt down with a smile and took my hand:
"When you open your eyes, child, where does it go?"
I ran away laughing, for I didn't know.

As I've grown older, the sun has set
On that strange land; and sometimes, I even forget
How it felt to roam free through the fields of my mind,
And be lost in the paradise I've left behind.

The Wanderers

I heard the Wanderers call first late one night,
Woeful and wild, as I lay curled tight
In my blankets; and I wept, for I was afraid
Of the life that shaped men who such fell noises made.

My mother came hurrying, sang sweet and low:
"Hush, child. Sleep, child. Wherever you go,
May the Lord love and keep you," and she tucked me in tight;
But her prayer rang so hollow as I tossed through the night.

I should've grown strong, but I was pale and withdrawn.
Troubled by strange dreams, I teetered, forlorn,
Between youth and manhood – was I waiting to ripen?
Was I waiting? Were they waiting? When they came, I was open.

The Wanderers came, a summons in their call;
Stood forth: raw, shrivelled, crippled, but powerful.
Their eyes shone like minerals out of used, quarried faces,
With a pure light that fills – heals – even as it pierces.

And they took me by hand, and called – called me by name;
Tore my long years of silence apart, and I scream.
My mother comes running; but stops dead, petrified.
As I try to move towards her, she dodges aside.

And then my father is there. We lock eyes. He's an animal;
The smell of his fear is heady and primal.
A mist comes on me, and I give myself over.
I come to in a world far removed; and it's over.

A restless touch in your sleep at night;
A gleam in the eyes that's a little too bright;
A prayer that rings false, and a calling inside you
To deface the masks that disfigure and hide you,

And stand naked to God. I was called, and I follow.
Hear my voice, meet my gaze; tell me my prayer rings hollow.
Are you naked as I? Are you truth, flesh, and blood?
I'm a Wanderer. I follow my call unto God.

You Alone

No church is Holy,
No temple, sacred.
There's no human blessing;
No rite is binding.

There's neither Hell, nor judgement.
Sin is but a feeling;
And though prophets move among us,
The last word is never spoken.

For each new life is born to freedom,
And all here have their calling:
Each heart's sacred chamber
Is a place of revelation.

No calendar can tell us
The day of our great meeting;
No saviour stand up in our place
As, one by one, and face-to-face
With God, we speak the Words of Grace.

No church is Holy.
There's no religion
But faith in God
As known to you;

And you alone.

Martyr's Wine

The truth pours from his mouth
Runs down his chin
Stains the white marble floor:
Sweet martyr's wine, sweet martyr's wine.

His body crumples and falls
Arms flung wildly in prayer.
A spirit, the spirit
Leaves him in a whisper

That flies round the hall,
Brushes each hidden heart
And dissolves, into silence.
Words deeper than thought,

Words no tongue can form
Drip from the dead man's mouth –
Tick. Tick. Tick. On the cold stone floor:
The secrets of faith.

Certainty

Certainty's an iron blessing
If you're of them who fear the truth;
Who call it freedom to be left guessing
In an Eden of eternal youth.
  Are you of them whose eyes are closed
  For fear of fear itself exposed?
  Do you *want* to know what you're repressing?
  Certainty's an iron blessing.

Knowledge is a cross to carry,
And a willing crucifixion.
A prophet's death, his crowning glory;
His suffering, a benediction –
  And in each heart's untrammelled deep
  An unborn prophet lies asleep.
  One day, he'll be crowned in glory;
  'til then, the cross is yours to carry.

Are you denial or acknowledgement?
Does your conscience, screened by walls of doubt,
Still call itself an innocent?
Are you listening, or drowning out?
  Blessed those who hear their calling;
  Who live for truths deeper than feeling.
  Your innermost truth is Heaven-sent.
  Are you denial or acknowledgement?

Reverie

Fall still, and hear the silence of our fading time:
The ringing in the ears of prayers unspoken;
The white noise of human lives stretched and broken;
The roar of our loveless god without name.

Fall still, and let the fabric of our waking dream
Weave itself through all you think and feel;
Open for the truths which only dreams reveal –
Join our reverie of lost time. Fall still.

Do you hear, in the music of the earth and sky,
The calling of the heart, and the spirit's soft reply?
A voice that sweeps this darkness; a breath; a whispered sigh
That says: *He who truly lives shall never die*?

Fall still, and let a timeless peace descend;
Let sanity settle on hearts crazed and broken.
The night air is heavy; the spirit has spoken.
Join in silence, together: feel our shattered lives mend.

Ending

A day of grace, a day of mercy
Breaks over this wasted land;
Spreads on our jagged horizon,
Heralds a new faith near at hand.

From ageless slumber, hearts are stirring;
Throbbing gently deep within
The breasts of animals and children.
They feel the new light on their skin.

And phantoms who spread fear among us
Burn up in the sun's bright glare;
Gleam like morning mist, and vanish –
Gone like they were never there.

There's no revelation, fire, nor judgement:
An elegiac peace descends.
A new day fills the sky with colour
As, here on earth, a cycle ends.

New Times

Like rain on every roof
Like wind in every tree
Like ash to every fire
The new times are coming.

Like lines on every face,
Like dreams in each young heart
That love fills and consumes,
The new times are coming.

Let go of memory,
Let go even of hope;
Of precious life itself, let go –
The new times are coming.

Give your empty heart
To be filled with the Spirit of Life.
All else must be consumed.
The new times are coming.

And when your fluttering heart falls still,
None shall grieve; but rejoice
To hear the Spirit of Life sing out:
"The New Times are Coming!"

Free Spirits

We blaze trails through the new disorder
The Earth is our state, and death, our border.

We cross the future's wild ground
By neither past nor present bound

Searching in hope. Will to live
Renewed at every step; *more* alive

And warmer; more human; freer;
We chase shadows by the light of that fire

For which our hearts were made to burn.
Walk with us. The clock hands turn;

Dance over their swirling blades –
New time's forming, old time fades.

Hear our song of life unborn;
Rise up to meet the new day's dawn:

We blaze trails through the new disorder
The Earth is our state; and death, our border.

Vision

Northern lights over London,
Northern lights for the blinded

Piercing the city glare
Like diamantine engine flare,

Rending its polluted veil;
Skyscrapers lashed by the livewire trail

As the solar winds flash through the skies.
Raise your head, you hopeless;

Open for revelation –
A new time's inauguration

In the blaze of new midnight:
The river-green, milk-white

Aurora. Rise over London
Like birds of a bright day;

Flare free wings, weightless,
Fly northwards and find us:

We, who were born with the new hope,
For whom the new time is soon ripe.

Follow our lights over London;
Our lights for the blinded.

Candles

The guiding light,
Through fields of cloud,
Through lifeless mist
On forgetting's lake of shadows;

The fading light,
A ghost who flits
Through haunted days,
Cloaked in a dream of pure tomorrows;

A prick of light
Between the graves:
Hear the bells
As it splits into a thousand glinting candles.

The light of God.
One by one
Our souls divide
Into a thousand glinting candles.

White Flame

Some hearts burn with a white flame,
Burn hotter than anger and shame.
Some spirits walk in a ring of light
Leading the blind through perpetual night;
Some hearts burn with a white flame.

And their souls blaze up for a great hope
Beyond even the truth towards which we grope:
That one day God may find
The lost and give sight to the blind;
And their souls blaze up with a white flame.

But as the night grows long, their light shines low.
As their aura fades to a shimmering glow,
The dying fire flares up, for an instant;
To clean the shadows from God's face, for an instant –
As their hearts burn out with a white flame.

Family

The friction of two bodies in the dark
Ignites the flame of life, the living spark
In hearts of darkness; kindles a new light,
Sending shadows rippling softly through the night.

Two spirits seal a pact of flesh and blood;
Of silent growth, of birth, of childhood:
Two free spirits, bound together to the grave
In endless celebration of the life they gave.

Over the newborn crying in her cot
Stand two tired watchers: pale, eyes bloodshot.
They look on, in wonder; and love, heart and soul,
The child whose coming made their family whole.

Birth

In the bitter distance
I hear my own lost songs.
I hear my fading voice.
I watch my proud form crumple.

Night comes crashing round me.
I see as through a white film
The mist of laboured breathing;
All the colours of emotion.

I watch myself lay dying,
Wrapped in folds of velvet silence.
My last prayer, mouthed and swallowed:
I taste the bitter resignation.

Shouldn't he have lived forever?
I can feel the distance calling.
I can hear a woman shrieking.
Must this carry on forever?

I turn away and leave him.
In my lungs a new day blossoms;
And I rise to meet it, singing.
A mother's shrieking ceases:

Her child is born.

Hearts of Stone

Chiselled in to hearts of stone,
The words of grace:
Thou shalt love, and be reborn
To living peace;
To tenderness; to life in hope
Of life without end.

The words of grace in hearts of stone;
A truth of spirit, flesh, and bone:
One neither lives, nor dies, alone.

Chiselled in our hearts of stone,
The mark of God:
Thou shalt love. Thou shalt love,
Suffer, and be glad.
Live in faith; a life in hope
Of life without end.

Storm

Are you my God
Who fills this shrouded sky?
Here, in the tempest's eye,
I feel you watching.

Are you my God?
Wrapped in this wild night,
This darkness glazed with light;
I feel you there.

Come fill my heart
With chaos and with love.
Your face shines high above:
I know you're watching.

My God, my God;
Reach out and take my hand.
Come claim me where I stand.
I feel you there.

Vacuum

They're the same stars;
The same distant fires
That lace the same skies;
Deaf to the same sighs,
Dry to the same tears:
The same vacuum of prayers.

The mirrored night
Shines with a shared fate;
Hope shines bright
In the mirrored night –
The same hope, the same love
Fills the vacuum above;

The same as when God
In a sudden spark, said:
"Stars, fires, skies, tears,
Night, fate, love, prayers,"
Whispered: "Humans. Free will."
And gave us a vacuum to fill.

Garden

There's a meeting place beyond the clouds,
A garden of fates and souls, where love's decided.
Join me there a while, by arches, ferns and running water;
Walk with me, rest with me. I'm waiting there.

Through the leaves whisper our true names;
White sculptures dance in perfect forms
Around a fountain of tears; there's an altar
Inscribed with thanks for answered prayers.

Shall we love? How shall we love?
Kneel by my side, and let us pray together:
We'll lay our lives in the hands of loving truth,
And the truth of our love will be decided.

I'm by the altar of fates and souls beyond the clouds.
Come and join me. Come and join me. I'll be waiting.

Angel

I flew on the wings of my dark days
High over my hometown's brickwork maze
On feathers red with sorrow, gold with grief;
I rose up on the wind of my failing life.

I rose to a great height, and I saw
The patterns of minutes and hours writ clear
On the earth's worn skin. I rose to the sublime;
And beheld beneath the mosaic of perfect time.

Then, a wave of cold, celestial light
Dyed my dark wings marble white;
Cleansed me of all earthly loss and fear.
I rose up, through Heaven's highest sphere,

Where, as an angel, I conversed with God.
She flew to meet me; flesh and blood.
Transformed, I circled down to earth:
A witness of salvation and rebirth.

Spirit

No longer to search, but to witness;

No longer to chase, but to carry;

No longer to fear, but to comfort;

No longer to consume, but to nourish;

Lost no longer, but a calling to others:

Reborn in Spirit. No longer alone.

Fields of Ash

Clad in joy, we walk the grey fields shining;
Side by side, our lives slowly entwining,

Sowing the chaos of a shared tomorrow
In fields of ash, fields of common sorrow.

The spirit lives within us, and is pure.
Mourners of a dead God; grieve no more.

Credo

I recognise the existence of God in my own life,
And in the lives of all those with whom I've come into contact.

I believe that God is love; love is God incarnate;
And that the highest human expression of divinity is unconditional love.

I consider the practice of faith to be a matter of individual conscience,
And I consider the spiritual freedom of the individual to be absolute.

I do not believe that the works of God
   can be understood or interpreted by mankind;
But that the true relationship between mankind and God is one of prayer.

I believe that a human being is, at the core of its being, a prayer.
I believe that human life itself is an act of faith.

PILGRIMAGE

A Book of Meditations

City

The city is as dust upon my skin. Its cold shadows cling to me as I wade through a swell of discordant voices. I was born here, but do not belong here. Who belongs here? Who is even welcome?

I am dizzy with the restlessness inside me; the same restlessness that stirs in all of us now as we try to settle further and further from our natural home. How long can we inhabit these tainted places? How much further can we travel on their straight concrete paths?

Restlessness and dissonance are spreading silently through us. The tremendous weight of the city on the soil beneath us is the pressure in our chests, the hard shell sucking at our hearts.

A restless voice will come at night and speak the truth of what is happening. That day, I will wash the dust of the city from my skin, and turn back to the elements that first created me.

Behind me, and all who go with me, I can already hear the buildings beginning to disintegrate in a cacophony of silence.

Pilgrimage

I crossed into the mountains slowly, feeling their hard skin knotted under my bootsoles, and the drag of their breath on my cheeks. I could see, at last, that I was completely alone; and my circling thoughts fell still.

Minutelessly, hourlessly, day and night came twice as I moved through a landscape of stony fields, climbing up onto a plateau. I walked steadily, aware of the sun inching through the sky overhead: it was as though I could feel the impossible speed with which the earth is turning.

On the third day, I had lain down beside a small brook to rest when I was startled by a plough of grey geese, passing northwards, right above me. They flew noiselessly, with the focus of long-distance travellers, and I watched them cross the broad plains of the sky and dip below the horizon. For a long time after they were gone, I lay still, imagining the air rippling outwards from the thrusts of their wings.

There was little else to fasten my thoughts upon; just smooth stone faces curving into one another, and a quiet which hung over the landscape like a low mist. I began to feel disorientated, checking and double-checking my bearings: they read right, but a dim sense that I was lost kept welling up in me. There were moments where I felt I should be swallowed by these strange, calm mountains—and moments where I felt I had no greater wish—but each time, I stood still a second, gathered my courage, and kept on. And, on the fifth day, the level curve of the horizon finally broke.

As I topped a small ridge, the high ground of the plateau fell away sharply; the skyline itself scrolling down, scrolled away beneath my feet. Looking outwards, I felt that I could take another step into the empty air, and that my free will alone would carry me. I could see the flight of mountain birds below me; and—if I am honest—for the long minutes that I stood there, I felt myself a god.

I sat down on the slope and took a meal, gazing out over the cliffs, and a river-valley wending its way between them. The exhilaration soon faded, and my spirits fell. What had become of the hopes I had brought to these mountains? Of secrets and revelations, knowledge and wisdom? I had written some prayers on my journey, and I prayed now; but when I rose and took the gravel path down towards the valley, there was loss and desolation in my heart.

I came down below the treeline as evening drew in. I was worn out, in body and spirit, and I began to cast about for a place to light a fire—the first for many days—and to sleep. A pair of crows flitted through the trees ahead of me, and I felt glad; relieved to have come down from the higher, lifeless altitudes.

I made for what looked to be a spit of flat ground where the birch trees seemed denser; but, as I drew closer, a deep gulley in the rock—perhaps thirty metres back and fifteen across—came into view. I beat a path through the vegetation, and stepped out into a clearing between three high cliff walls; invisible from the path, but with a wide view over the valley. By the rim of the cliff stood a stool made of thin stumps bound crudely together, and a ring of charred stones. I slung my pack to the ground and began to gather wood, pleased for this first sign of human habitation. Soon, a lively blaze sprang up between the stones; the dry birchwood cracking and popping merrily.

The nights in the warmer months of the year never grow dark in this part of the world; and I sat, sunk in thought, as a silver-blue twilight filled the valley. For a long time, I stared mutely into the distance, and into the fire, filled with a sweet homesickness for the city streets of my childhood; a longing that had been dormant many years. Only when my stock of firewood was exhausted, did I get up to look for a softer strip of ground on which to pass the night.

It was then that I saw the mouth of the cave in the back of the gulley; where the lips of the rock had been peeled back over a gaping hole, sucking in the twilight. I was at once struck by a kind of vertigo: of horror, blended with searing, sickening, hope.

As though compelled, I stepped forward, until my face was pressed up against that yawning blackness. I waited, a long moment, until all feeling in me had fallen still; then stepped, boldly, three, four paces into the cave.

Turning, I could see the entrance: a soft, shimmering portal behind me; and that was all. I stood, listening. After a time, I sat; the floor was surprisingly smooth, and at length I lay down, on my back, feeling my heartbeat pulse through my entire body. The darkness seeped into me; it was like the darkness of a mother's flesh, and warmed me. Neither awake nor asleep, but dreaming vividly, I passed the night.

When morning came, sunlight poured in through the mouth of the cave and I could see it had been lived in, for there was stone furniture: a table, a place to sit, and a lattice of branches in the corner which must once have served as a bed.

I came out into the daylight and fetched my notebook, whereupon I began to write; recording from the experience of my senses the voices I had heard, and the visions I had seen.

Mountains

Mountains sleep beneath our feet in the summer. The thirsty roots of bushes and birch trees suck the life from them, and the heavy stone sinks down upon itself, enervated, dozing calmly as the season's hikers sigh and groan in wonder.

The eyelids of a mountain flutter as the first leaves fall. Their eyes of stone glow in the darkness: through the long autumn nights, they open to gaze lovingly up at the stars. The mountain's face is swept by the jealous wind; shorn smooth for the kiss of the first snow.

But the autumn is a time of patience. The hands of earth and sky brush, tenderly, in the banks of low cloud. The rain falls, but runs off in streams and rivulets; and on the next clear night the mountains and stars are left gazing at one another: filled with longing, but distant as before.

Then, on a still day, cold and tranquil, the stars will fall as snow. The arms of the mountains are spread wide, and the soft body of the heavens sinks slowly into their broad embrace. "How can you hold me, all of me, how?" each snowflake whispers. "I can hold all of you, all of you," the mountains whisper back; and next morning, the sky and the stone rest cheek to cheek against one another: harmonious, loving, and peaceful.

But love is a season; and, year upon year, the stars trickle away. They glitter in the mountain becks and creeks as they flow back to the ocean, where they twinkle in the eye of a smiling god, pleased to watch the serious play of his creation. The mountains are left bare, and slowly fall back into their dreaming sleep, letting leaves and shrubs grow to screen the press of the light upon tired eyelids. The first bold hikers can hear the dreams of mountains, if their ears are attuned to the deeper frequencies of the earth and stars; but soon, they are drowned out by the cries of animal, bird, and man.

The mountain's sleep grows deeper as the summer approaches.

Peak

Where once I saw a reflection of myself in the faces of others; I now recognise, in everyone I meet, that which I can only call God.

When I first sought God, I discovered that I was blind to myself; that all I had found in my self-seeking was vanity and illusion. I began to see unsuspected depths and heights in others; and I learned that only very few were aware of their greater dimensions.

There were many who perceived dimly that I could see them, and bade me come closer. I stood at the foot of many mountains, and climbed a little way into the foothills to where I could see their towering peaks, and the sky beyond the peaks; and I threw many warm words into cold wells and abysses, standing long and waiting patiently for an echo.

And I was at my deepest at the foot of others' heights, and at my most lofty standing over their chasms. I was at my most stable amidst the earthquakes and eruptions by which they were formed.

And over every peak I saw the same sky; in every chasm, the same darkness; and the sun and the moon danced above me, wherever I stood. This sky and this darkness, I call God. This sun and this moon I call the living God, whose day begins at birth and night at the hour of death.

Do I, too, have such heights, such chasms; and do the sun and the moon follow their course over my life, also?

The soft light in your eyes tells me this is so.

Sky

The spirit is a bird with thin wings: for some, a tern; for some, a swift; for some, a swallow.

Consciousness is a sky strewn with clouded thoughts; a sky without borders through which our spirits flit: calling to one another, gliding wing-to-wing, gathered high up in a great flock; or solitary, swerving and diving, never landing, skimming the waters off life's grey coast.

Look up, and see our two spirits circling overhead. Though one day, our bodies will crumple and be laid to rest in the ground, our spirits will weave tirelessly through this sky without borders. They'll dart between the clouds of others' thoughts; they'll call out with the voice of freedom into others' silence.

In the way that bird and sky are joined in flight; our spirits, in prayer, become eternal.

Flight

A spirit is a caged bird. Its plumage glitters many colours, but its wings remain folded and tailfeathers tucked in, until man grows bold enough to open the door of its cage.

The spirit can only hop and limp at first, for it has never flown; only dreamed of flying though the long captivity of childhood and youth. It totters about on spindly legs, stretching its wings; and seems, to any onlooker, ridiculous and pathetic.

Its first flight is that of a house bird, in quick circles around the furniture. But soon, as its confidence grows, it begins to flit restlessly from perch to perch; sensing, perhaps, the potential of the sky in the small thrusts of its wings.

Until man opens a window—and out it soars! The first flight into open skies is a moment of great joy for the spirit: it understands, finally, why it has wings; and that its wings must grow broad and strong to carry it high over rooftops and mountains.

It soars high: dangerously high. Gripped by a sudden fear of heights, it flaps in alarm back in through the window, crawls into its cage, and draws its shimmering wings down over its face. Even the spirits which have become most free once suffered from this fear of flying.

But the spirit is, by nature, brave; and gathers courage for a new attempt. And now it is away from man a long, long time, as it loses itself in the wholeness and emptiness of the sky. Man's house, meanwhile, is cold and quiet. He begins to fear that he has been abandoned. It is only when he opens his own door and steps outside, standing for the first time under heaven, that he again discovers his spirit: a speck, circling in the far distance.

Seeing man appear under the sky, the spirit remembers his face and glides down, majestically, to perch on a branch in man's garden. There, man and his spirit can exist in harmony, and pass many hours together. Man—who cannot live in the open, endless sky—keeps his home and his bed and his groundedness; and the spirit, never to return to its cage or fold its wings beneath a roof, can fly freely, and return again to man, whom it loves.

Wingtips curled finely as eyelashes, bold colours glittering on its feathers in the sunlight, the spirit has become a magnificent creature; and it has both a fierce cry, and a melodious song. How many of the secrets of man were first heard in this cry, and this song? How much was first seen by a watchful, solitary spirit, circling overhead?

Water

At the source of my being is a pool of still water;
  Pure water, that quenches my every thirst.
I know nothing of myself that I have not seen as a reflection on its surface.
I know nothing of God that I did not first find in its depth.

However hard the winds blow in the treetops above me,
  The water does not ripple.
However cold the air when winter comes, the water does not freeze.

I am baptised here again and again each morning;
  And, as I emerge naked from the water,
The stains on my hands and the taint on my soul are washed away.

Lighthouse

In this age where so many are adrift and searching, clutching on to wrecks and scraps to stay afloat, the few who wash up on land are bound, by their humanity, to become the lighthouse keepers.

I built my lighthouse on a hilltop not far from the great city. A lighthouse for all those who, standing under the streetlights at the city's perimeter, might gaze out into the darkness and see its flickering, living flame raised over the ridgeline; and at the sight of this flame know that darkness is not emptiness; that there exists a beyond; that theirs is not the only and inevitable form of existence.

I built my lighthouse close to the city, to tell the desperate mankind that's formed there that the ring of light and concrete which surrounds them *can* be broken.

Perhaps someone, strengthened by this knowledge, will find the courage to take their first step out into the darkness.

Blind

The luminescence of faith is like sunlight on the skin of the blind.

There are no paths marked by lanterns and signposts for the faithful; no junctions between good and evil; no gates and no borders between heaven and hell. These white skies are deaf to your confessions, and you have to carry your burdens wherever you travel in search of God.

The way of faith runs through the darkest wildernesses of the human heart; where, enveloped in a cloud of your own lovelessness and vanity, you lift your gaze seeking guidance—and recognise nothing. Where you will be seized by fear of the unknown, though you are not lost. Go calmly further, and you will again feel the kiss of sunlight upon your forehead.

Go willingly into the darkness; let it fill you. Light follows darkness as surely as day follows night, and the luminescence of faith is like sunlight on the skin of the blind.

Go blind, and do not be afraid.

Ring

Closing my eyes, I see a crowd of men, women, and angels.

The men and women stand meekly in an outer ring, heads bowed and hands folded, praying in silence.

Angels, wearing our human clothes and faces, but evanescent, like doused light, or glowing shadows, fill the ring: meeting, embracing in warmth and laughter, with all the grace of our human spirits freed from the bonds of ever having existed on earth.

Fear, shame, pity, judgement, envy, ill-will, and hatred stand silent in a ring, heads bowed meekly; whilst love dances with itself in their midst, naked and jubilant.

And our shared will to love one another is realised, for a few short seconds. When I open my eyes, I am one in a ring of weathered faces looking into one another shyly; alive with openness and wonder.

Tyamaro

There was a man called Tyamaro. He lived alone, on the cliffs of an ancient sea, and he had turned his back upon the world in order to be closer to God. Men from the villages believed he was a prophet: they brought him food, and begged him to speak to them, to guide them in the affairs of their lives.

Tyamaro listened patiently to all those who climbed the cliffs to his hut. His replies were cryptic, and he said little; but he had an aura of warmth and calm that settled on his visitors, and they returned to their own cares and hardships filled with new resolve.

The older men from the villages loved and respected Tyamaro. Although they were never sure that they understood all that he had told them, they believed that whatever he said was true. Gradually, as these old men grew ill and died, it became tradition among them to ask Tyamaro to scatter their ashes from his cliffs, in the hope that their souls would be at peace when they came to rest in God's hand.

The married men did not visit Tyamaro often—only upon the death of a parent, or the birth of a child—but still they felt that Tyamaro belonged to them; that he was as much a part of their community as the shepherds or the boatsmen. It was they who took turns to lay a basket of olives and bread crusts at Tyamaro's door each morning.

But one night, a disagreement arose amongst the young men of the villages; most of whom had never spoken to Tyamaro, except at the insistence of their fathers. They were afraid of him, and did not like the way his grey-green eyes seemed to peer into their hearts. All that lay hidden there seemed twice as painful, twice as bitter, after meeting Tyamaro; and for this, many of them nurtured a secret hatred of the man their fathers and grandfathers revered as a man of God.

A group of these young men met together in a hut on the shoreline. They drank, and their tongues grew looser. When they came to speak of Tyamaro, several of them became angry: cursing, branding him a charlatan and a parasite. There was a roar of approval, and when two of the youngest boys—who had been raised by their grandfathers and loved Tyamaro dearly—stood up to defend him, they were shouted down.

The next morning, Tyamaro was found dead in his hut, with one long gash from his chin to his chest.

There was a trial, and the two who had spoken out to defend Tyamaro bore witness against those who had slandered him. These men, twelve in all, denounced one another in the same way they had denounced Tyamaro, and each declared his remorse that he had spoken so rashly. No-one came forward and confessed, and there was no way for the elder judge to discern the guilt or innocence of any of these twelve men, for their word could not be trusted.

Judgement was felled at dawn the following day. The twelve men were, on pain of exile, each to carry a large stone from the foot of the bay to Tyamaro's dwelling on the cliffs, every morning. There, they were to build, first an altar, then a monument to his memory that should tower high over the cliffs in bright stone, as a marker for ships and caravans for miles around. The young men accepted their judgement meekly, with their heads bowed.

For many years, all twelve of them rose with the dawn and bore their stones to Tyamaro's altar, which became a holy place for the people of the villages, and Tyamaro's monument rose up slowly from the ground. As rumour spread, pilgrims made the journey from distant cities to lay a stone—or a precious jewel—at his grave.

Slowly, grief lifted from the hearts of the villagers who had known Tyamaro. They looked up towards his spire on the ridgeline and felt that his life had not been in vain. "Tyamaro" became a word in their language, meaning truthfulness, or purity; and it was the only word of their language that foreign travellers knew and understood.

The shame and remorse of the eleven who had spoken out against Tyamaro also faded. The elder judge passed away; the crime of Tyamaro's murder was gradually accepted, and then forgotten. They began to carry their stones less often: first every third day, then every week, then every month; until it was only on feastdays that they would take a white pebble from the beach and lay it at the foot of Tyamaro's monument, at the head of a long procession.

The twelfth man was a poor goatherd, who lived alone. Every day, without fail, he continued to rise at dawn, climb the cliffs, and lay his stone at Tyamaro's altar. From this, the people of the villages knew that it was he who had killed Tyamaro; but no word was spoken against him, even by the men who had shared his punishment. He was looked upon with deep respect, for a transformation had taken place within him. Those who remembered Tyamaro—there were many now living in the villages who did not—swore that this goatherd had, in the course of the years, acquired something of the aura of gentleness and nobility of Tyamaro himself.

But time passed; and the goatherd, too, grew old. When his legs would no longer carry him up the steep road from the bay to the cliffs, the task of bearing his stone was passed on to the brightest youth of the villages, as a sign that they had come of age. To this day, those who make the pilgrimage to Tyamaro's monument can see, each dawn, a youth come, touch his forehead to the alter, lay his stone reverently, and descend again from the cliffs. To this day, this is a holy place, where ashes are scattered and crying babies are brought under the eyes of God. The word "Tyamaro," in many languages, has come to mean not only truthfulness, and purity; but also prayer.

Adam

Six thousand; sixty thousand; six hundred thousand years ago—or whenever it was—a cluster of people sat grouped around a fire in the warm weather, chatting in dead languages about the harvest, the peace, the governor, the neighbours, and everything under the sun.

One of the group reclines slightly, resting his rugged palms on the logs stacked up behind him, as he lets the conversation, and the crackling of the fire, wash over him. His work for the day is done, and his mind wanders; his gaze passing gently over the faces of the others in this small community, relaxing into their shared lives. The chatter grows louder; a serious, sharper tone edges in for a second, before dissolving in a ripple of laughter.

Animals. They realise nothing. Life is a circumstance; instincts are dominant; meaning is survival. Taking care of one another because they must, they work together just as their mothers and fathers did; and every innovation, every technology that has changed their lives and the scope of their lives, has done nothing to alter their fundamental mode of existence. Man as animal. In all its glory.

His gaze comes to rest on the weathered face of a man opposite, a face he's seen a thousand times before. He's seen this other man work, sleep, watched him kill, fall in love, cry, heard him sing; and all of this is written clearly into the other man's features: a beautiful animal. His gaze lingers: the shadows of the fire throw the contours of the face into shadow; the light of the fire dancing in the other man's eyes.

Their gazes meet; they stare into one another. The first man's eyes widen, slightly, and his mouth opens. His companion grins at him, but he doesn't respond. For he's seen it. In the set of the other man's shoulders and neck; the working muscles of his expression as he's talking; in the hollows of his eyes—most of all in his eyes, in his pupils. All of them, there, around the fire: in the other man's eyes. The man's mother and father. His own mother, father, and children. His ancestors. *Their* ancestors; their descendants, down to the present day, in their—in our—essential form; dancing in the other man's eyes.

"Adam!"

The group gathers around him, concerned; but he comes to, dazed, and stumbles to his feet, brushing aside their outstretched hands. Wordless, with a deep absence in his features and movements, he lurches away from the fire, and off into the darkness. The others curse at him and laugh; he seems not to notice. Full, with their humanity; bursting, with humanity, he staggers away.

That light. That light! Anything, to douse it; any shadow deep enough to drink all of it in, to the last drop, that the world might sink back down into the darkness. Trees hide the moon: it grows brighter. Eyes screwed tight shut: it grows brighter, blinding. The animal searches inside himself for his own shadow, his own darkness—for he, too, has suffered and caused others to suffer, has killed and denied and hated—but there, the light is most piercing of all, and he is forced to open himself that the light may leave his body; for it comes from within, and is consuming him. Opening, he is radiant, and all shadows flee from him.

And he became human: his animal nature recast in a new mould. The light came into his eyes, dancing there, night and day, and his open gaze was feared, for it was piercing; but those who opened themselves to him were filled with his spirit and walked the earth as humanity, with light in their eyes and knowledge in their hearts. They fought, and killed, and cast long shadows over one another, just as before; but the light with its source in the shadow shone fiercely, undiminished.

We fight, and kill, and cast long shadows over one another, just as before; but the light and the knowledge with its source in the shadow shine from us, undiminished, to this day.

Pilgrim

The air around me trembled with the words of my calling; the elements whispered, begging and commanding me to listen. A voice far above and a voice within sang out, in perfect harmony; and one by one, the crowd of my own voices fell still.

I was filled with the riddle and the secret of God, resonant with the music of an infinite being, singing without voice, as I will never sing again.

Now, I am guided by the calling within me. I have left to travel to where the air is the breath of God and the ground the palm of God's hand. My spirit has begun its long wandering, and there is no longer any place here on earth I can call home.

Threshold

I walk the passage of time to the boundary of fate, where my body and my spirit will part.

My body will be borne further on its bier by loving hands, and laid to rest in the ground.

My spirit will dissolve into the Spirit of Life from whence it came, like a silk cloth unravelling in a clouded sky; the threads of my personality unwinding as my funeral hymns are sung.

But the Spirit of Life is eternal, and I walk the passage of time in expectation of eternal life. My own being must necessarily and irrevocably dissolve; but life lives further, and the Spirit of Life further still, to ignite a new living spark even after many lifeless ages.

At the threshold of fate, I will bow my head and release the Spirit of Life within me, with a prayer.

Clarity

There comes a time in every person's life when the Spirit of Life within them is most concentrated, and purest: when they are most alive, strongest, and their existence has extended to its outermost bounds.

Clarity is the essence of this time. One can see, as through a mirror, one's coming weakness; one's dissolution; one's mortality; and the coming weakness and dissolution of all things.

One can see, as in a mirror, one's birth from nothing; one's entire history; and the birth of all things from nothing—the original act of creation.

At this time of enlightenment, one's will is most free.

How well prepared were you? How well prepared will you be for this sudden freedom? Did you grasp it? Will it slip through your fingers and disappear, like memory after a funeral in a mist of moving life?

To what end, your greatest freedom?

To what end, your most profound act upon this earth?

Silence

Freedom is the silence in which you can hear your true calling.

It is not a keeping silent, nor the silent weeping of repressed voices. It is not the silence of expectation before a crowd, or of deafness; nor a busy, working silence; nor the softer wordlessness of lovers and friends.

First in the silence of prayer are the senses attuned to what, for every person, is their higher calling.

Sink deep into a prayerful silence: where your day and your night, your doing and your thinking, your humanity, and the fulfilment of your basic needs, all become a part of your offering unto God.

Not to say a prayer, but to become yourself a prayer, is the way to freedom.

For in prayerful silence which cannot be broken, you will hear the words of your true calling chiming in your ears, and in your heart: your freedom is to answer.

Religion

You, whose faith is deep and whose prayers are resonant, must go and keep company with our siblings who have neither faith, nor prayers of their own.

There are many among them who would pray, but do not know how. You cannot teach them. You must not seek to lead them in your rituals, to your truth. Share your beliefs and your rituals with them, with the same meekness as were it they who were sharing the deepest secrets of their lives with you.

Recall for them your own journey beneath the false bottom of your personality, and above the glass ceiling of your ambitions. Give generously of your own experiences, and of yourself; and not in the expectation of gratitude: give of your gratitude. The opportunity to share your most profound experience with another is its own reward.

Speak so that others can hear you. Listen so that others can be sure they have been heard. And teach of nothing but freedom: freedom of religion; freedom of conscience; freedom of worship. My prayer is that others will have faith in your teaching, go forth, and, after your example, discover for themselves the form of prayer and worship that is entirely their own.

Mistaken

There are as many conflicting interpretations of the nature of God as there are ripples on the surface of the history of mankind.

To those who would disagree with what I have written, I would say that an understanding of the nature of God is every person's property: it is an individual's birthright, and their only birthright. It follows that the nature of God is a topic on which anyone is qualified to express themselves. However, I have one condition for anybody who would compare their views with mine.

Let the person who would disagree with me be certain of their own claims. So certain that, when their darkest day comes and the heaviest shadows are thrown upon them, they know that even then, as their time on earth passes its nadir, their certainty will not waver.

And so certain that, when they stand at the pinnacle of their life, the air is thin, and they have furthest to fall, they know that they will look out over the broadest horizons they will ever see on earth, and see nothing over which to be surprised.

If, having arrived at such certainty, we meet to discuss the nature of God, and we do not part as brothers; then it is I who was mistaken.

Crucifixion[1]

On a hill outside Jerusalem, an armed guard escorts a man bearing a thick wooden cross to his place of execution. A crowd of several thousand has gathered to march with them: most are hostile, cursing and spitting; others weeping; others silent. The man's body is young, but years of poverty have left him shrivelled; his cheeks are sallow from long hours of torture. He has a pure, unsettling light in his eyes.

The procession climbs slowly towards the ridgeline, the crack of a whip cutting through the clamour now and then as the man with the cross falters: his strength is failing. Eventually, he sinks to his knees, and though the whip strikes his bare back—twice—and a third time—he remains unmoving. His guards gather to confer, before they pull a man from the crowd at random and fasten the cross to his shoulders; striking at him with redoubled fury until his protests cease, and he begins to walk. The procession continues until the crowd is gathered at the highest point on the ridge. The first man is bound by his wrists, and dragged behind.

Three men are to be executed. All three are tied down and then nailed to their wooden frames, and all three give off the same howl as the nails are driven through them. Their crosses are hoisted, slotted into deep grooves in the rock, and then pegged down, though the day is muggy and windless. The soldiers work in silence, and soon, all three men hang there, gloriously. The crowd is restive, and seems almost to throb with a bulging, silent hate. Hate for the soldiers; hate for the condemned men; hate for themselves, and one another: all are complicit. Everyone's a witness.

The silence stretches. The bodies of the three men suspended on their crosses hang limp, life ebbing from them. The man with the light in his eyes, in the middle, turns to the pasty, gruesome man hanging to his left.

"God have mercy on you."

---

1. The quotations in the penultimate paragraph of this text are from Friedrich Nietzsche, *Thus Spoke Zarathustra* (London: Penguin, 1961) Translated by R. J. Hollingdale.

Without hesitation the man turns his pallid face away, pressing his cheek hard into the wood.

Thereafter he turns to the man on his right, who is younger, and emanates panic and a sort of desperate cunning.

"God have mercy on you," he says, again, with a cracked, bloodied voice that makes the words sound almost vicious. The other man looks into his eyes, but there's not the slightest change in his expression; it's not clear whether he has heard, or understood.

"God have mercy on you!"

The shout rings out from the crowd, incredulous, hate-filled, and others quickly chime in. They howl, and heckle, until the noise swells and bubbles over into violence. Fists are shaken, stones hurled, buttons, coins, anything to hand is thrown in fury at the three men hanging defenceless, a metre and a half in the air. A slab of granite hits the man on the left on the temple, and he is knocked out. All three men are streaked with the blood of new wounds, as the roar of hate subsides.

Hours later, the crowd has kept its vigil, and is undiminished. One of the men has died: the younger, much of his strength spent in a kind of feverish resistance. The man with the light in his eyes is also dying. For a long time, he has hung there, immobile; his only vital sign the heaving of his chest. But he opens his eyes, then, slowly, meeting the gaze of person after person in the crowd, as though searching for something.

"My God."

He was still looking into the faces of the people gathered at his feet, and the soldiers, but no longer searching. He spoke with the greatest dignity, with no trace of complaint or suffering.

"My God."

"Why have you forsaken me?"

His gaze lost focus. The light faded from it. He closed his eyes.

I heard an answer deep within me, resonating inside me; and I opened my mouth, and gave voice:

"Man is something that shall be overcome."
"Man is something that shall be overcome."
"Man is something that shall be overcome."

"And God is dead: for we have killed him."

The silence was complete. The man passed away, and the people gathered there turned to look at me. The presence within me fled, and I stood silent, drinking in their sheer animal complexity. And then I broke their silence with a laugh: cold, ironic, and powerful. Somebody out there understood, and our laughter rang out together; and soon, the whole crowd was laughing along with us, relieved.

PRAYERS

For the Blinded

God, lead the blinded back to themselves in the darkness.
Guide them back to us through the darkness.
Gather them to you, so their darkness
Becomes a pebble in an ocean of light.

For Travellers

God, those who travel with a question,
May they find clarity;
Those who travel with a burden,
May they find release;
Those who travel blind,
Give them the courage to be guided by their hearts.
Wherever we set our course, whatever has inspired us,
God, be with us as we travel.

For Those Left Waiting

God, we who are waiting live half-heartedly:
Only in our prayers can we be whole.
Let the call to prayer resonate through our hollow expectations.
Bring our lives to prayer.
Bring our prayers to life.

For Those Carrying a Cross

God, never let us forget why we took up the crosses we carry.
Be there, when we sink to our knees.
Be there, when our strength returns.
Be there, when we arrive, to relieve us of our burdens.

For Strength

God, may we find humility in our own weakness,
And, through humility, self-respect. May self-respect
Become a source of tolerance,
And the habits of tolerance build our strength.
May life, in its infinity of forms, grow stronger.

For the Proud

God, humble us. Reunite us with the all-consuming life
From which we were formed;
Through which we are reformed;
Into which we must one day dissolve.

For the Pitiful

God, show yourself to us in the gaze of the pitiful.
Bring our hardened hearts, through pity,
To an understanding of our own impotence and powerlessness
In the face of the suffering in this world.

For Those in Debt

God, help us to accept that we all stand in debt to one another:
The rich to the poor;
The strong to the weak;
The fulfilled to the loveless.
Give us the courage to share our goods,
And the humility to share our burdens.

For Innocence

God, each morning and each evening awaken the memory of childhood.
May the first and the last moments of each day be innocent;
Even as we walk our paths with sunken shoulders,
Bowed under the weight of a cross.

For the Prejudiced

God, free us from dead tradition and prejudice.
Break through the barriers
Which segregate individuals and peoples here on earth
And broaden our hearts, that all humanity may claim its place therein.

For Reconciliation

God, we lift our hearts over the strife which divides us.
Reconcile us, that we may come together once again.

For Those Who Love

God, bind as family all those who love one another.
Help us sculpt a future in the image of the love we have inside us,
In which we can be together with the people in whose love we share.

For Those with Strong Feelings

God, bring our feelings to fulfilment in the bonds we share with others.
May the strength and depth of our feelings
Become our strength, through tolerance,
And our depth, through forgiveness. God, never let us forget
That love is the root of all feeling.

For Those with Hidden Longing

God, give those with a longing inside them the courage
To open themselves to the world.
Give us the wisdom to respect their calling:
To accept both the need, and the fulfilment, of others as our own.

For the Restless

God, lift our restlessness over our own narrow purposes.
Free us from our ambitions, our desires,
And fill with love that which is unfulfilled inside us:
Love for others, in which we can rest.

For the Anxious

God, although the uncertainty in which we live can be a burden,
Help us see it as the proof of development and change.
Bring forth in us the inspiration that is the source of all anxiety
And the sense of justice that is the root of our unease.

For Those in Doubt

God, accept our doubt as part of the balance of faith;
As the humanity of faith. Bless our doubt
With the knowledge that it can only be completely resolved
Once our lives have come to an end.

For Those Who Are Afraid

God, we who are afraid of the light, afraid of exposure,
Afraid of our own falsehood and impurity,
Afraid of a shadowed life, afraid of death;
Call us to you with music. Bring our fear
Into harmony with all fear.

For the Tense

God, send inspiration to release the tension building inside us.
Guide us as we bring tension to expression as change,
As we reforge our inner lives
In harmony with the lives of those around us.

For Those Under Pressure

God, be with us as our lives transform.
Be the unchangeable element within us:
Our kernel when, under pressure,
We're driven deeper inside ourselves,
And our dreams are stripped away.

For the Desperate

God, may we be overwhelmed by our need
And may it transform us.
Bring us to the pure source of our desperation
And let us kneel, and drink.

For Those in Crisis

God, push us over the brink and show us a new dimension:
May your chaos and our order resolve into a greater whole.
Give us the courage to be open at the point of crisis,
As you enter into our lives.

For Those in Freefall

God, help those who are falling fall tenderly.
Help them accept the pull to earth as the pull back to life:
To fold their arms and fall, trusting
That you'll be there with them, picking up the pieces,
Once they've hit the ground.

For Humanity

God, preserve our human nature as life transforms around us.
Let the blood that has been spilt sink into the Earth.
Give us the courage to forgive, to love, and to be human.

For Hope

God, beautify us with happiness, deepen us with sorrow;
Unravel our hearts through laughter, and bind them through passion.
May memory sleep peacefully within us, dreaming of hope.

For the Creative

God, bless the work of our hands;
Be with those who create in the spirit of prayer.
May all our works carry the seed of our own creation.

For Life Everlasting

God, fill our lives with your eternal spirit.
Give voice to eternity through our words and music;
Sculpt the image of eternity with our hands.
May the light of the hope of everlasting life shine from us
   as long as we live.

Amen

www.ingramcontent.com/pod-product-compliance
Lightning Source LLC
Chambersburg PA
CBHW060651150426

42813CB00052B/583